Cathedral of the Hand

poems by

Dianna MacKinnon Henning

Finishing Line Press
Georgetown, Kentucky

Cathedral of the Hand

ACKNOWLEDGMENTS

AESTHETICA, UK, CREATIVE WRITING ANNUAL, (FINALIST): "BETWEEN
YOUNG AND OLD TIME": LONGLISTED FOR "BETWEEN YOUNG AND OLD
TIME," PUBLISHED IN *AESTHETICA'S ANNUAL*
CALIFORNIA QUARTERLY: "WHEN A DAY TRIPS YOU UP, SPITS YOU OUT"
CLACKAMAS LITERARY REVIEW: "CHAIRBED"
CONVERGENCE: "THINGS THAT KEEP US APART"
FUTURECYCLE: "THE ONE WITH VIOLETS IN HER LAP"
HAWAI'I PACIFIC REVIEW: "THE BUTCHER'S APPRENTICE," (NOMINATED
FOR PUSHCART)
LUMMOX: "NEEDING BREAD," & "ONCE"
PSYCHOLOGICAL PERSPECTIVES, A QUARTERLY JOURNAL OF JUNGIAN
THOUGHT: "LITTLE HOUSE THAT SLEEPS UNDERNEATH WINTER'S
MOON"
THE MAIN STREET RAG: "HOUSE OF UMBRELLAS" & "THE STEP INTO
HOUSE"
A YEAR OF BEING HERE: "SET FREE," "WHEN THE HUMMING BIRD'S BEAK
CAUGHT IN THE WINDOW SCREEN"
POETRY NOW: "Dogs at Midnight Underneath the Moon" (Editor's Choice)

Editor: Christen Kincaid

Cover Art: Jody Wright

Author Photo: Kam Vento

Cover Design: Elizabeth Maines

Printed in the USA on acid-free paper.
Order online: www.finishinglinepress.com
also available on amazon.com

Author inquiries and mail orders:
Finishing Line Press
P. O. Box 1626
Georgetown, Kentucky 40324
U. S. A.

Table of Contents

*For my Sisters, Miriam Aiken Robinson & Manjula Leggett,
& Jody Wright*

When in the Long Ago

There was a woman
who lived beneath the sea
and each day
the whole day through
she wove a cloth from water

Each evening when she lay aside
her work, the tides
followed their course,
and unraveled
all she had done

By the following day
the very same woman
beneath the sea
began again

She never complained
as she sat at her loom,
the splendid slips of water
spinning through her fingers

For Jane Kenyon

Her hand is a cup the gods drink from,
and when they finish,
they brush their pale lips
across the centerfold of her palm,
the smell of her skin,
ripe olives in the sun.

Look at the way she bends
closer as if to hear
their smallest utterance,
her attention so fine, so keen.

What is it that she tells them
in a resonant voice,
that they should endlessly stand
without once flinching?

What She Tells Them

> *"A sound commences in my left ear/like the sound of the sea in a shell." "After an Illness, Walking the dog."* —Jane Kenyon

She speaks of the sea,
of depths beyond belief,
of shrouded bones,
and words diaphanous as air,
of star-catchers in their bright tunics.

She does not speak of the stone
lodged in her head,
its cold appeal, its terrible weight,
nor how she took it as her betrothed.

The heaviness in her heart
tethers her to earth,
and although the stone
cuts deep into memory's grain,
the lavender tongue still speaks.

Skin of the Elder

Didn't her old hands smell of the sea,
as you cupped them to your cheeks?

Weren't those blue-veined hands ancient,
somehow exotic? You'd run your forefinger

down the furrowed frontside of her hand,
her life flowing into you.

Isn't that the way you memorialized ancestors,
tracking them back to yourself

so that future generations would know
hand-bridges span distance;

the same way a river sometimes runs its course
to empty into the ocean?

Turning into Spring at Winter's Start

In the crimson blaze of cuffed leaves
scattered by wind

and late migratory flocks,
scent of winter seeps through our walls,

the house damp and its chill a reminder
to stack wood, fetch kindling.

I think of a loved one set to earth,
the shovel's heavy work,

and wonder if my friend heard what I caught—
crows so masterful, their chorus

split the hour in which we stood graveside.
Those cheeky birds pecked

freshly dug mounds for seedlings,
while we held hands for steady footing.

The One with Violets in Her Lap
(Title from Sappho)

If she were someone else's sister
I would make her mine,
twist her bones
into recognition—
the catacombs of her eyes,
deep and memorable.

If she were lost
I would surely find her,
coax her back,
the same way she returned
with each push
on the playground swing.

My studio clock,
a mercenary,
intones its message.

She won't return.

The one who survives
is the one left behind.

Set Free

When my husband caught the trapped hummingbird
and freed it from the screened-in porch,
his big hands, a bird's nest,
a few fingers opened into an escape hatch,

I held my breath as one does before the delicate—
that spot of bird, singular in its journey,
wings like small lead windows.

It seemed strange to see a big man
who could easily crush the body of such a small thing
release to air the hummingbird, who once in flight,
turned as if to say, I'll remember this.

When the Hummingbird's Beak Caught in the Window Screen

the tiny thing tried to back up,
if one can call reversing gears release,

its beak so finely wedded to the screen,
although threaded might be more appropriate;

nonetheless, its nervous hovering
remained until the nail of its beak broke loose

and off the bird took, flash of wings a blur,
the teeny god headed towards its own mystery,

and not once did it explain its fear
or utter anything about a harrowing escape.

Cathedral of the Hand

The hand touches things of this world
and transforms them.
It's no accident that the face of God is in the palm.

What the hand would do for world peace
is seldom mentioned
in the larger colony of hands.

(No gunshot, no bombs to rupture the countryside.)
The hand could be an angel if it tried.
See how the fingers open like wings.

Between Young and Old Time

I am reading a book loaned to me by a very old woman.
Her hands are on the pages and they are slipping into mine;
flesh of a book against my brow as I close my eyes to rest.

What I love best about this book recommended by an old woman,
is how a single strand of silver hair becomes my bookmark—
between two pages, a single strand of hair shows where I left off.

Where I left off is not where I am or where I intend to be.
Further into the book than ever imagined is a story about being
an old woman who reads a book and recognizes herself

in a character. The old woman looks out from the book,
an old woman's eyes large as an oasis and clear as sunlit sand.
Her hand is a vine of many veins that intertwine and signal
    something.

Something close and dear as song expresses itself on her lips.
She is sipping lyrics from the air through the straw of a strand of hair.
Her hands are on the pages and they are slipping into mine.

The Butcher's Apprentice

First he was shown how to hold the cleaver,
where to make the best cut
and how beautifully the meat opened,
gracious host to its own body.
The apprentice wiped his hands
across his white apron;
his sigh, such finesse, a sigh
a lover might make after climax,
but no climax here,
only the calm of knowing
one did the other body right,
and can't you tell
that the one being trained
sought the best advice,
especially since fine butchery
is nearly extinct,
for why else would the Master
train the hand coming back to fingers,
to open, carefully at first,
the red inner flesh that was once desire.

Beyond the Fence

a buck stops to rest, tail swatting flies, nose glossy as though
recently stream-dipped, only there are no streams,
this our fourth year of drought,
a nearby creek skeletal with rocks.

I imagine the buck sucking leaves that are still green
late September, gnashing out whatever liquid remains.

Whatever moves him to travel along this trail, to finally rest
in a hollowed out bed of dry grasses, to at last close
his eyes over this season of absolute dryness,

must be whatever entices us to sleep side-by-side
in the blue-black dark where the hours drip their minutes;
where by morning we age into something new.

Dogs at Midnight Underneath the Moon

When we tottered out to check on our barking dogs,
nothing suspect lurked in the dark, so our drowsy hearts
sashayed their usual waltz until we saw our malamutes'
eyes ablaze, their fur razed,

as though both dogs
had battled intruders off the premises.
The moon rested her head on the pond's lap
while the malamutes circled and re-circled its muddy banks.

Each time the canines dipped their tongues,
they first stopped to bark as though

multiple dogs were reflected
in the stillness of water. But our multiple lives are not
too much, especially when the moon sends us her white lilies.

Forgot Our Field Glasses Back Home

An eagle drew our eyes upward
into the half burned tree, its branches sparse
as a hatchling's feathers, and then the rain,
a soggy slather, broke through our sight,
as well as admiration for the moment
which romped off so suddenly
you questioned what we'd seen;
a bird, tree limb or neither,
and we hustled for the car
where everything oozed wet,
me fondly reminiscing the bird
we'd seen—you pronouncing it a branch.

Once

we scudded smooth-bellied stones across the lake,
counted their skips and starts to see who won.

Who is winning now is anyone's guess,
a beefy sun beating down our backs;
the memory-stone stuck in swampy dregs.

I would like to remember you as you were,
tall, handsome, taut with sex—
about to slip out of your skin.

But memory is a dicey thing,
a stone that sinks
to settle where it can't easily be seen.

Red House by Covered Bridge

It was empty, so we ran around the house hoping to find
a way in; cornflakes of paint peeling off the front door. Inside,

we saw our lives: Chairs by the woodstove,
you reading *The New York Times*,
your feet on a footrest. We would need to strip
off wallpaper that belonged

to another century, repaint the outside to protect the weathered,
tender wood. And tender were we when first married, feast of flesh,

salty taste of the good. We walked to the bridge; headed down-
hill to dip our feet in water so cold we yelped and hustled back

to the picnic blanket we'd earlier spread. Was it Chianti we drank,
or ripple? The years peel from their framework
of time, and although

we never bought that place we live there still. I am writing this
to tell you, The covered bridge was simply a way
to get over the river.

When a Day Trips You up, Spits You Out

There are times when you leave your house and are organized,
and other days when even the post-mistress frowns;
chastising you—your mailings
too bulky and poorly packaged, another
submission returned "postage due."
On such days even the rusted lilacs near the post's front door
droop like crumpled hankies.
Ok, you say, I'll drive home and re-do what they
wouldn't take. But the new mailers balk
at your stuffing them and perhaps
you are trying to fill what feels empty inside,
the tape clogged into a sticky mass.
Not one to give up, you hop back in the car
with your manila envelopes,
postage-due money pocketed.
When the post-mistress sees you, she says:
"Dear, you're a mess today. Your shirt's undone."
A man standing in another line confirms this,
adds, "Great view," and you gasp. Then back home
that poem you've worked so hard on dares you
in its most obnoxious voice to toss it, start a new one.

The Step into House

In your dreams it waits there like an absent thought.
The walkway is strewn with leaves
and the steps lead into memory.
Who are you girl, entering that house?
Not a scrap of sound spilling from underneath its door.

Girl-child trying to lead an adult's life.
You simply couldn't help it. Sex was just too big.
Then you got big. Pregnant big. Had several children,
all of whom moved with you into the Step Into House.

It was not a readymade dwelling. You had to grow up
before the house-key was turned over, improvements made.
The rooms were pastures where your children grazed.
Plenty of hay in the kitchen where the kettle bubbled.

Who is that knocking now, you might ask?
None other than yourself, come home.
It was a very long way, the journey filled with travails and joy.
You dieted on tears, tore open loaves of laughter.
There are many things a house can hold. Love is one of them.

House of Umbrellas

Your family boasted a particular genius for tar-paper.
There was nothing they couldn't cover up with it.

The world is black simply because it is dark.
A match blown out, a candle's dormant wick.

Your fingers read the news off cracks in the roof—
they follow the sound of trouble breaking through:

tar-paper snaps free, scatters on the ground—
debris to be hauled off after the rain.

No matter how many umbrellas are raised,
slippage still seeps through. It isn't what
darkness hides; it's what's hidden in the heart.

In the hierarchy of broken things, someone's sleeping
takes up a room for the night. Water splashes off her face.

She cannot hold what cannot be contained.

No Firm Deal

My mother's body is the house from which I was born.
There were no umbrellas, nothing to keep
the womb's water from washing over me.

I wasn't born a fish because fish
are not part of my genetic makeup.

When I stare into my dog's eyes,
I'm jettisoned into eternity.
That is quite a place, infinite in magnitude.

I am not infinite; yet hope to become so when I pass.
One can only wish for an afterlife.

There is no firm deal in prayers.

Reading the Lives

You sketch the rooms onto your bare knee.
Always, the houses are old,
far older than you, and a dusting of other lives fill
that space once occupied: the bedroom where Grandmother
spilled her Maja Powder; a kitchen counter
where pie dough was rolled onto a snowfield of flour;
your father's dreams buried in dust,
their musty afterlife taking up residence inside you.

Lilacs might romance the air,
so that you think of yourself as many people
entering your front door, eating with you at supper;
you, as Dale Evans in cowgirl clothes,
sometimes Emily Dickinson, your white dress
skimming the toe of your *Mary Jane's*. In one of the houses,
wind streams through lax window casings,
while the basement's coal furnace bellows—
always a dirge for someone in your home,
your sister's casket on display in the living room.

And there are happy rooms, rooms that nearly splash
with sunlight, you and your cousins at charades,
the eldest cousin, a new-age Davy Crockett,
and you dressed in a bed sheet acting out Snow White.

Some rooms open a page at a time,
and you read the lives that once lived there,
their closets filled with regret,
your father's outlines for patents tarnished yellow,
rolled into scrolls, paper clipped and set aside;
you left behind reading the dead.

Old House on East Empire St.

Our house was not as large as when we
lived there, the bedrooms
barely big enough for a bed and double chest.
And the kitchen floor's
heating grate where we stood to warm in winter
revealed only the dark
beneath the grill. Was it always dark? What of
the times when we

called the room our Happy Kitchen?
Memory. What an irascible
scoundrel. If we were happy we failed
to make mention. Pity.
What was good was enough while
it lasted. I went back to ask
the new owners to see our old home.
Even the walls eavesdropped

on whatever thoughts meandered my head.
It was awful, wasn't it?
We were, for a while, nearly perfection. Whose fault?
Then you strayed
and I likewise. Chafe a face long enough
and bruising starts to appear.
Who called it quits? Doesn't matter.
Our kitchen was only an excuse to be more.

Things that Keep Us from One Another

Let's suppose distance was never about mileage,
or the wear and tear on tires, rather it was about attitude,
how leaving home meant leaving behind everything familiar.

It was never about gas prices or packing and luggage.
Rather, it was about how sunshine pours through the bedroom
window and makes wall silhouettes off the flowers,

the house well rehearsed in art's solace;
how it sedates one into feeling secure—
even the floor mapping a way for feet that nightly

stumble to the bathroom. No, you once said,
you couldn't visit because the house, your own
house, kept you captive; so much to do: rearrange

furniture because with the living room's new paint
nothing looked right; clean the garage to find the right tool,
patch the guest-house where a snow plow jabbed cedar siding.

Let me tell you we miss you and would love you to visit.
We cannot quite remember your kiss on our cheeks,
or the way your arrival makes the house dance.

Little House That Sleeps
Underneath Winter's Moon

A squall of creamy light glazes the cedar
siding of our house. Late from town, I fumble

for my keys; the cats nabbed by sleep,
purring in their languid coats on the Adirondack

chair. Whatever exists beyond the ponderosa
pines stands like sentinels, muffled in the near-

dark, branches sketched on moonlit snow. To tell the truth,
I want to linger at my door, search for my keys

for hours and watch how the moon masters our house,
each nuance made greater by mysterious light.

Chairbed

Such ecstasy when the chairs met
face to face and you tucked pillows in,
spread out your blessing blanket,
climbed aboard your life.

From the doorway the hickory straight-backs
looked like school chums
about to knock fists,
but instead hold back.

Beyond the window screen,
summer's careening birds,
rustle of rabbits and partridge.

Hickory was perfect wood for other worlds,
until the Elders argued chairs
are nothing more than seats,
and took apart what you'd carefully made.

Needing Bread

My hunger is nothing
compared to my intent.
Yeast makes things rise: even
the dead climb up from their graves.

Tins of dough wait by the stove
like stubborn mules.
But they won't bray
once they're in the oven.

There's no way to explain
the mastery of bread-making.
It requires one straighten the spine,
push down what's risen.

Clover

Before rising into the foliage of my life, I was honey,
something extracted and poured into another,
so that when you found me there was no resemblance
to my former self, the person you thought I was,
a façade. I jotted notes on where

next to retrieve myself. Across forever-
fields filled with wild flowers, someone like myself
spent days, searching through clover,
especially for the illusive four-leafed one
to snap in a locket—the Celtic cross above my heart.

A teacher once said shamrocks bring luck
and luck is more than *Keep at something long enough*
and the gold of art becomes revelation.

In all honesty, my former name escapes me.

Let's face it; becoming a self is hard work,
and one cannot be outfoxed.

Now I call myself Clover.

At the Center

I skim the roadside for animals. The air smells of pine.
It is the fox and her mate I most hope to see.

Once my dog treed a fox that shut its eyes as we drew near.
Like when a child with shuteyes believes he can't be seen.
—Dusk, and the trees dim to sticks of charcoal.

I do not want to be seen on this night.
I want to become the air the fox breathes.
Because I am alone inside myself
the wind carries me.

It is good to live with the foxes and animals.
They are the ones born at the center of the universe.

The Story of El Capitan
by Jody Wright

The Yosemite area was originally inhabited by the Miwok Indians. This is the folktale they told to explain why they called the mountain Tutokanula. Mother Bear's two cubs strayed from her one day and, after playing in the Merced River, fell fast asleep atop a rock. As they slept, the rock kept growing until it touched the clouds. Mother Bear searched high and low for them, and although none of the animals she asked had seen them, they said they would help her look. A hawk passing over the now towering rock saw the sleeping cubs and flew down to let Mother Bear know. Mother Bear tried climbing the rock but did not get far. As she despaired, tiny measuring worm told her it would go up to get them. The other animals scoffed to think that such a tiny creature could save the cubs. One by one, they all tried to climb the mountain, but all failed. Again the measuring worm said it would try. Mother Bear thanked it, and the measuring worm began its slow climb. As its body stretched out, it sang *tu,* and as it scrunched up, it sang *tok.* All the way up, it sang *tu-tok, tu-tok.* After days of this, it finally reached the cubs, which it gently woke. Very slowly they inched their way back down, the younger cub following the older cub, which was following the inch worm. Never again did the animals laugh at the measuring worm for being so small. They had learned that doing great things has nothing to do with one's size. That is why the Miwok Indians called the towering rock *"Tutokanula,"* which means "Measuring Worm Mountain" in their language.

Additional Acknowledgements

Books: *The Tenderness House*, Poet's Corner Press," 2004 & *The Broken Bone Tongue*, Black Buzzard Press, 2009 & Y/Historical Novel, *Seasoning the Blade*, 2013, Lucky Bat Books

Thanks to The California Council for the Humanities Stories Project for a ('08) grant that funded poetry workshops at the Rancheria in Susanville where I worked with Maidu, Pit River, Washoe and the Northern Paiute Tribes. Also thanks to the California Arts Council for their "Artists in the Schools Residency," funded, in part, by The National Endowment for the Arts and The William James Association's Prison Arts Program & California Poets in the Schools.

A special thank you to the Thompson Peak Writers' Workshop Participants, Christen Kincaid, and Lynn Pedersen

"BENEATH ALL THIS I'M CARVING A CATHEDRAL/ OF SALT." –NICK FLYNN

M̲s. Henning was born and raised in Vermont, a land close to her heart, and which she visits as often as possible. *Vermont is in my blood,* she says. Dianna holds an MFA from Vermont College of Fine Arts. Published in, in part: *The Main Street Rag, Crazyhorse, The Lullwater Review, California Quarterly, Poetry International, Fugue, The Tule Review, The Asheville Poetry Review, Clackamas Literary Review, South Dakota Review, Hawai'i Pacific Review* and *The Seattle Review.* Nominated for 3 Pushcarts. Won fellowships to Bread Loaf and Dublin Writers' Center. Finalist in Aesthetica's Creative Writing Award in the UK, published in their Annual 2014. Dianna taught for California Poets in the Schools, and through the William James Association's Prison Arts Project, as well as being a recipient of several California Arts Council grants which allowed her to teach at the Stockton Youth Authority and at Diamond View School in Susanville.

Dianna lives in Lassen County on six acres with her husband Kam and her malamute Sakari. She also facilitates The Thompson Peak Writers' Workshop in Lassen County.

Website: www.diannahenning.com